Celtic Saints
of WESSEX

Elizabeth Rees

Contents

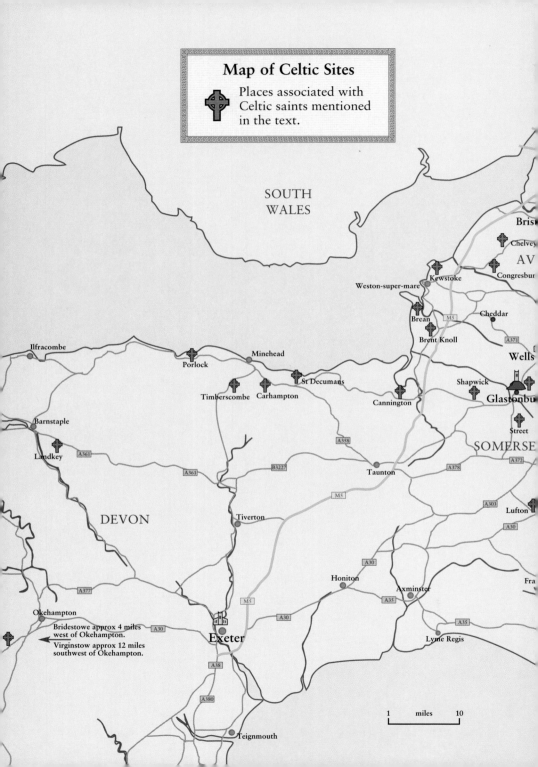

Map of Celtic Sites

Places associated with Celtic saints mentioned in the text.

SOUTH WALES

BRIS

Chelvey

AV

Congresbur

Kewstoke

Weston-super-mare

Cheddar

Brean

M5

A371

Brent Knoll

Ilfracombe

Wells

Minehead

Porlock

St Decumans

Shapwick

Timberscombe   Carhampton

Glastonbu

Cannington

Barnstaple

Street

Landkey

A361

SOMERSE

A358

A372

A361

B3227

A378

Taunton

M5

A303

Lufton

DEVON

Tiverton

A30

A30

A377

Honiton

Axminster

Fra

M5

A35

A35

Okehampton

Bridestowe approx 4 miles
west of Okehampton.

A30

Virginstow approx 12 miles
southwest of Okehampton.

Exeter

Lyme Regis

A38

A380

1   miles   10

Teignmouth

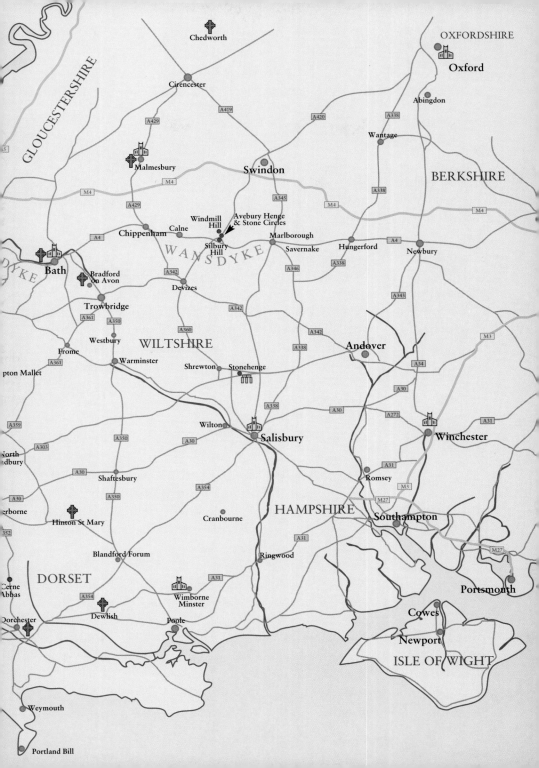

1 *In the beginning:* Romano–British Christians in the towns

There is little evidence of the presence of early Christians in Wessex, but a considerable number of clues survive. The name Wessex denotes the area conquered by the West Saxons, which includes parts of Wiltshire, Dorset, Gloucestershire, Devon and Somerset. Throughout this region, archaeology provides us with information about the life and worship of the early British Christians whom the Saxons conquered.

Bath (Somerset): a healing centre where Christians are first named

Our first reference to Christians in Britain comes in the unlikely form of a prayer to a pagan goddess who was worshipped in Bath. In Roman times, Bath was a famous centre for healing. Its hot spring of mineral water in the deep valley of the River Avon, now in the centre of Bath, had long been a subject of wonder to ancient people. It emerged into a marshy pool, overhung with steam on winter days.

By the first century BC, this area was ruled by the Celtic tribe of the Dobuni, who believed that the spring was sacred to the goddess Sulis. In AD 44 the holy site was swallowed up in the heavily patrolled military zone beside the Fosse Way, which ran from Exeter to Lincoln. In about AD 60, the Roman authorities turned the native sanctuary of Sulis into a magnificent healing centre. They enclosed the spring within a massive reservoir, lined with sheets of lead from the Mendips, and made the ground stable with oak piles. They quarried limestone from the Downs overlooking the site, to build a complex of baths and temples.[1]

Bath was now known as *Aquae Sulis* ('The Waters of Sulis'). Visitors came here from mainland Europe: France, Spain and Germany. They equated Sulis with the Roman goddess Minerva. Such conflation of deities was common in the Roman provinces: it appeased native feeling, made obscure local cults intelligible to visitors, and reassured those who believed in the classical pantheon.

OPPOSITE:
A Roman channel conveys the steaming water from the reservoir to the great bath.

Fourth-century visitors to the wondrous hot springs and the temple of Sulis Minerva followed the custom of the time by writing requests to the goddess on small, rolled-up sheets of pewter: about 130 of these were excavated by Barry Cunliffe in 1978–80. Many are difficult to decipher because they were written backwards, or in code. Some of these 'curse tablets' (or *defixiones*) were thrown into the healing waters; most of them asked the goddess to punish someone for theft. One of these was written by or for a supplicant named Annianus, who was angry because someone had stolen six silver coins from his purse that very morning. He wanted Sulis to recover his money from this pickpocket.

The text of his curse begins: 'Whether pagan or Christian, whosoever, whether man or woman, whether boy or girl, whether slave or free has stolen from me, Annianus, in the morning, six silver pieces from my purse, you lady Goddess, are to exact [them] from him.' It lists eighteen suspects. Although found at a pagan shrine, the author's use of the phrase 'pagan or Christian' implies that when it was written, Christianity occupied a distinct position in society that other religions did not.[2]

Excavations in Walcot Street, Bath, in the year 2000 revealed the graves of a man and a woman who may have been Christians. The two graves were oriented east–west; one contained the first lead coffin to be found in Bath, in which was the body of a man aged about 45, possibly a wealthy trader. The other grave contained the wooden coffin of a woman aged around 30, of slightly lower rank. The two late fourth-century burials were set against the wall of an imposing yet decaying Roman town house with colonnades, beside Walcot Street, the busy road at the north end of Bath, leading eastwards towards London. The absence of grave goods and the east–west orientation of the graves suggests that these

were Christians living at the end of the period of Roman occupation of Bath.[3] Did Annianus know this couple?

From AD 367 onwards, barbarians attacked Britain. Villas were destroyed and their inhabitants thrown down wells; people fled from the cities. In Bath the temple and the baths became increasingly derelict. In an eighth-century Anglo-Saxon poem, a monk laments the ruin of the town. He describes the destruction of the bath complex and the tiles falling from its curved roof:

> There stood courts of stone with a gushing spring
> of boiling water in welling floods...
> The roofs are in ruin, the towers are wrecked,
> the frost-covered bastions battered and fallen . . .

The drainage system broke down, and gradually the water rose, until black mud covered everything.

Yet the spring continued to flow, and the shrine continued to be held holy. In 675, Osric, King of the Hwicce, a sub-kingdom of Mercia, granted land to Abbess Berta to establish a convent of nuns at Bath. In 757–8 we hear of land being made over to the monks of St Peter's church. It is likely that these two communities lived near the centre of the town, close to the spring. Saxon burials have been found just north of the spring, above the east end of the Roman baths.

Reconstruction of the pediment of the Roman temple in Bath. Two winged Victories support a central image of the local deity.

In the twelfth century, the Norman bishop John of Tours built a fine new abbey on the site. The monastic infirmary was constructed above the temple precinct to the north of the spring, and the Roman walls of the hall, which once enclosed the spring, were used to create a new bath fed by the hot spring.[4]

Shepton Mallet (Somerset): a priest's pendant is unearthed

One of Britain's earliest datable Christian artefacts was found eighteen miles southwest of Bath, where a small Roman town at Shepton Mallet perhaps serviced an as yet undiscovered garrison on the Fosse Way. Excavations in 1990 beside Fosse Lane on the edge of Shepton Mallet uncovered a large Roman home with a central courtyard and what may have been a half-timbered barn. A little to the south was a house with three rooms dating from the second century, with a smithy close by. Further south was a Christian cemetery, with seventeen bodies buried facing east–west, set within a ditched enclosure. Most of them were buried in wooden coffins set in graves cut from the rock. One is built of lead, and in another an amulet of silver alloy was found.

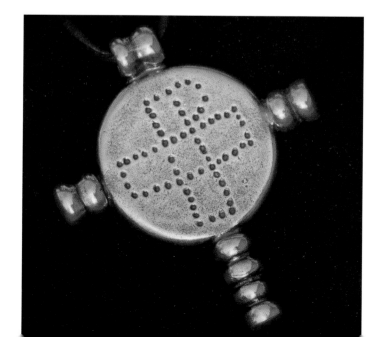

Replica of the amulet found at Shepton Mallet

The amulet is in the form of a disc with short, segmented arms, giving it the form of a cross. It has a loop at the top for the wearer to attach it to a chain round his neck. Crudely punched into it is a late form of the *chi-rho* monogram, the first two letters of the Greek word *Christos*. This unique pendant may have been worn by the community's priest. It is the latest datable object from the site, and was made soon after AD 400, about the time when the Romans were withdrawing from Britain.

Two smaller pagan cemeteries were uncovered, with their occupants buried north-south, a few of them decapitated. In a bigger town, cemeteries would have been outside the inhabited area, but here they are located within the settlement, and perhaps represented different social or family groups.[5] The fact that the Christian cemetery is the largest of the three suggests that this region was Christianised by the late fourth century. In 2004, excavation on the opposite side of the Fosse Way revealed shop frontages, with living spaces behind. One person had decorated his shop front by choosing a limestone slab adorned with a giant coiled ammonite. Builders decorate walls with fossils in the same way today.

Wessex is unique in that more early Christian cemeteries have been discovered in this region than anywhere else. One reason for this may be that the area was well populated in early times, while today much of the region is not built over, so that early sites have survived, and can be excavated. There was a very large cemetery at Poundbury outside Dorchester, between the River Frome and the main road leading northwest from the town of *Durnovaria*. Excavations between 1964 and 1980 uncovered over 1400 graves. A few date from the Iron Age and early Roman times, but most are late Roman, from the time when Christianity had become standard in the Roman empire. Most of the graves are aligned east–west; the

Early Christian cemeteries of Dorset and Somerset

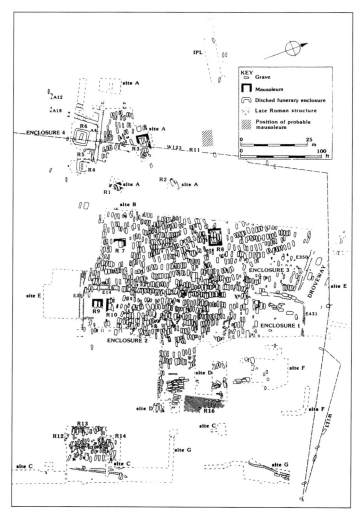

*Late Roman
Christian cemetery
at Poundbury,
Dorset*

bodies are buried in wooden coffins with very few grave goods. A few wealthier people were buried in stone- or lead-lined coffins, and there were at least eight small funeral chapels, decorated inside with painted wall plaster. These were probably commissioned by individual families, for several people were buried in each chapel. The graves and mausolea were arranged in orderly rows.[6]

At Cannington in Somerset there was a cemetery which remained in use until considerably later. The name Cannington means 'Quantock village'; this settlement lies at the foot of the Quantock Hills. In early times it was in an important location near the River Parrett, which provides access to the Bristol Channel. Its hill fort was occupied from late Roman times until the seventh or eighth century.

During excavations in 1962, 523 graves were examined on the hillside to the east of the fort, although many more had been destroyed by quarrying. The cemetery may have contained between two and five thousand burials, and there was a post-Roman settlement just outside the walls of the fort. The cemetery appears to have served a large populated area throughout Celtic times and into the Saxon period.[7]

Cannington cemetery's earliest burials date from the second century AD, and the burials appear to have been Christian from the sixth century onwards. A young woman whose grave was radiocarbon-dated to around AD 621 seems to have been a local Christian saint. Her grave was marked out from the others by a low mound, and stone had been brought from elsewhere, to build a memorial chapel over her tomb. There was evidence that her grave was frequently visited; her tomb provided a focus for many other burials.[8] She is one of the anonymous saints of the region, maybe a local nun. In the eighth century the population moved further south to the present village of Cannington.

Cannington hill fort

2 Christians in rural villas

OPPOSITE:

The mosaic floor from Hinton St Mary, now in the British Museum

While many Christians lived in Roman towns, others lived in villas in the countryside, and humbler folk were employed on their estates. In his autobiographical text, *The Confession*, St Patrick tells us that his father was both a villa owner and a deacon in the Romano–British church; his grandfather was a priest. When the Romans withdrew from Britain, a villa often became the nucleus of a village, as the name implies, and when the villa's owners were Christian, its chapel or burial ground might become the site of the village church.

Letters survive written by Christian clergy and laymen in fourth and fifth century Gaul, describing wealthy landowners who became bishops. It appears that after the collapse of central Roman authority, some owners of large estates in Gaul entered the Church, in order to legitimise their status and position. Many continued to live on their country estates, and turned part of the villa into a church serving the rural community. There are accounts of baptisteries within these villas, suggesting a lively Christian church, joined by new members.[9] We do not know what happened in Britain at this time, but a Christian chapel survives in Lullingstone villa in Kent, and Wessex provides further evidence of rural house churches.

House Churches in two Dorset villas: Frampton and Hinton St Mary

The two Roman villas of Frampton and Hinton St Mary are only fifteen miles away from one another; Frampton is four miles northwest of Dorchester. We know that both villas served as house churches because of their unique mosaic floors. That of Hinton St Mary was found in 1963; it dates from AD 350–355, and since most of the villa was destroyed, the mosaic was transferred to the British Museum. It is designed as a continuous floor in two large panels, to fit two connecting rooms. The larger of the two rooms faced east, as churches traditionally do. They face the rising sun, a symbol

*Roundel depicting
the head of Christ,
Roman mosaic,
Hinton St Mary*

of Christ rising from the darkness of death. The smaller room could be screened off with a wooden folding door, or by a heavy curtain suspended from an arch above the threshold. In this way candidates for baptism could be separated from the initiated Christians, who then gathered around the altar to share the Eucharist.[10]

At the centre of the larger room, in front of a *chi-rho* symbol, Christ is depicted as a youthful hero. He has a composed expression, and large, dark penetrating eyes. His head is flanked by pomegranates: these were a symbol of the resurrection, and refer to the Greek myth in which Persephone was taken to the underworld and ate six pomegranate seeds. For six months each year, she returned to life from the kingdom of the dead. In Christian tradition, pomegranates symbolised Christ's resurrection right up to the Renaissance, when Italian artists painted the Virgin Mary holding the infant Jesus who clasps a pomegranate as he ponders his future resurrection.

The heads and shoulders of human figures appear at each corner of this mosaic. People at this time believed that the earth was square, and the human figures are the four evangelists taking the good news of Christ to the four corners of the earth. With their locks of windswept red hair, they also represent the four winds.[11] Writing in about AD 185, St Irenaeus relates the number of the gospels to that of the four chief winds and the earth's four corners, to which the winds convey the life-giving message of the word of God.

Between the heads of the four evangelists are four half-circles, or lunettes. One at the eastern end depicts the tree of life in paradise; the other three contain lively scenes in which a hound chases or confronts a deer. No human hunters are depicted, and the hounds do not wound or kill the deer. In Christian art, a hunting scene represented our struggle with the forces of evil. One of the chief purposes of Roman domestic art was to provide an appropriate setting for philosophical discussions, poetry and literature, and so it is unlikely that we are reading too much into the symbolism of these villa mosaics.

If you turn the book upside down, you will see that in the smaller room the central roundel depicts the Greek hero Bellerophon mounted on his horse, Pegasus, slaying the three-headed monster, the Chimaera. This was a myth similar to the story of St George and the dragon: it symbolises Christ's struggle with evil and ours also. On each side, a panel depicts a hunting scene, like those surrounding the head of Christ. The catechumens, who probably stayed here during the Eucharist, were still struggling to rise with Christ at Easter.

In the larger room, the head of Christ occupies a central position of honour. Maybe the priest stood sideways on the mosaic panel between the two rooms during the Liturgy of the Word, praying with and reading to the people in both rooms. For the Liturgy of the Eucharist, a curtain might be drawn across, or a door closed. There is space for a portable altar between the panel and the image of Christ's head, where the mosaic is discoloured. The priest could stand behind the figure of Christ and face east as he celebrated the Eucharist surrounded by the baptised Christians. The people would look across the icon of Christ on the floor to the altar, where he was sacramentally present.[12]

The mosaic floors of Frampton's villa are now lost, but were carefully drawn by Samuel Lysons in 1813. Two of them

Mosaic floors, Frampton Roman villa, S.Lysons, 1813

are reproduced here. They came from the same workshop as the mosaics at Hinton St Mary. In both villas, the mosaics are closely ornamented, and not intended to be covered with dining room furniture. The designs are arranged to be viewed from different positions, and suggest a dynamic use of space involving movement, procession, and the designation of some spaces as more important than others.[13]

As the illustration shows, the larger room was shaped like a church. There was an apse facing east, with a *chi–rho* symbol occupying a place of honour on its threshold. During the

Eucharist, the priest would have stood before a portable altar in the apse, facing the gathered Christians across the *chi-rho* symbol of Christ. The apse was a powerful architectural feature: it represented a gateway to heaven, a sacred space set beneath a heavenly dome. Here, a large *cantharus* or chalice forms a centrepiece. This was originally the wine cup in which an aristocratic host mixed wine with water for his guests. By the mid-fourth century it symbolised the mixing of wine and water in the Eucharist.[14]

If you turn the picture round the opposite way, close to the *chi-rho* symbol but facing in the opposite direction, you can see a mask of Neptune, the water god. A Latin couplet describes his functions, and a procession of dolphins round the entire edge of the room converges on Neptune. In pagan art, Neptune and the sea beasts symbolised the voyage of the dead to the Isles of the Blest, and Christians adopted this imagery to depict the journey of the soul to paradise. We are dolphins swimming through the perilous sea of death to heaven. There are painted masks of Neptune in the Roman catacombs, and a representation of Neptune's trident accompanied by a procession of dolphins appears on a Christian sarcophagus discovered beneath the pavement of St Peter's in Rome. At the centre of the large room, a damaged roundel portrays Bellerophon's struggle against evil.[15]

The candidates for baptism probably withdrew to the side room, which may have been curtained off along the decorated panel, as at Hinton St Mary. In the central roundel of this room, where the catechumens spent the second half of the Eucharist learning more about their faith, the god Bacchus is depicted, riding a panther. Bacchus was understood as a saviour-god, a symbol of triumph over death and a blissful afterlife. For Christians, pagan myths were understood as hints foreshadowing the true revelation of Christ, and so there are painted masks of Bacchus in the catacombs. On either side of the Bacchus roundel at Frampton, a panel depicts a hunting scene, for the catechumens to ponder as they reflected on their own struggle with their pursuing sins.[16]

At the north end of Frampton villa there was another elaborate mosaic. At its four corners, the four evangelists are again depicted as the four winds. There is a hunting scene in which deer represent Christians pursued by the hounds of sin and pleasure. The mosaic's central figure is Neptune; dolphins reappear as souls sailing through the waters of baptism into everlasting life. The mosaic has borders of stylised waves, and is surrounded by light blue *tesserae*; with its watery theme, this may have been where converts were baptised.[17]

Pagans become Christians: Chedworth villa, Gloucestershire

Evidence from Chedworth villa suggests that Romano-Britons were also baptised in pools. Nine miles southeast of Cheltenham, Chedworth is situated at the head of the sheltered valley of the River Coln. It was occupied in the fourth century, and its owners became Christian at some point. The villa's source of water is a spring which flows through a *nymphaeum*, or shrine to the local water spirit, where it is contained in an octagonal pool surrounded by paving slabs.

An apsed shrine containing a small pagan altar was built over it. Three of the slabs which surrounded the pool have the *chi-rho* and other Christian symbols carved on them, so by then the pool was probably used to immerse candidates for baptism. Christianity may have been a passing phase, however, for later owners turned the slabs over and used them for other purposes.[18]

Archaeologist Graham Webster has suggested that Chedworth may have been a healing centre, since it appears to have too many rooms for a normal family villa, and a number

of altars were found here. With its *nymphaeum* and a nearby temple, pilgrims may have come here to bathe, sleep and receive healing dreams and advice. There were a number of such healing sanctuaries in the region. At Chedworth, perhaps the pagan priests were more skilful or experienced than their Christian counterparts.

Octagonal pool of the nymphaeum, *Chedworth Roman villa*

Early writings describe Christians being baptised in public baths, and we can guess that when a Roman villa became a house church, catechumens might be baptised in the bath suite of the villa. In the fourth century, monumental cold plunge baths were added to villas at Lufton near Yeovil (Somerset) and Dewlish, northeast of Dorchester (Dorset), each in octagonal form, like Chedworth's pool. In late antiquity, guests could be entertained in ornate bath-houses, so these impressive plunge baths might have been intended for secular purposes, but why were these cold plunges eight-sided, as baptisteries often were? According to St Ambrose, an octagonal baptistery symbolised the eight days of creation, in particular, the eighth day on which God rested, the Sabbath day of eternity, into which the new Christian entered.[19]

Britain's first post-Roman baptistery at Bradford-on-Avon, Wiltshire

As we saw at Frampton, baptism might also take place in the villa's living rooms. Excavations at the Roman villa of Bradford-on-Avon in 2003 revealed that a fifth-century Romano-British landowner converted the chief reception room of his stately home into an apsed chapel. He might have been the local priest, or indeed Bradford's bishop, since baptism was conducted by bishops at this time. This was a lavishly designed double villa dating from the mid third century, but after the withdrawal of the Romans from Britain, and the subsequent economic decline, money was becoming scarce, and the villa's owner built a rather simple baptistery on top of the fine mosaic floor of the reception room.

It consisted of a stone font surrounded by a low circular dry stone wall, which stood a metre high; it was built while the villa was still roofed. The baptistery's crude, unplastered finish contrasts poorly with the elaborate mosaic on which it stands. Within the circular enclosure, a font made of stone, lead, or even wood, was probably set into the floor. A shallow pit acted as a soak-away or drain. The font would be large enough to allow the candidate to stand knee deep in water, while the bishop poured water over his head. This post-Roman baptistery within a villa is unique in Britain, but there are parallels in fifth-century Gaul and Italy: there is a similar baptistery at Rennes in eastern Brittany.[20]

In contrast to the humble baptistery, the fine earlier mosaic on which it stands is reminiscent of those found in Tunisia, in north Africa. Its imagery recalls Christian themes, which suggests that the space may have initially been designed as a

Archaeology students from St Laurence School uncover the baptistery wall in the Roman villa, Bradford-on-Avon. The apse mosaic is visible.

Christian chapel. At the northern end of the mosaic in the apse is a *cantharus* or wine cup, flanked by dolphins representing human souls. This surmounts a square patterned area, at the centre of which a rosette, symbolising eternity, stands at the centre of an octagonal figure.

This chief room in the villa is approached from the outside by a pair of doors flanked by two pillars. The approach on the right side is worn down, in contrast to that on the left. This suggests that the left door was kept shut, and that the faithful approached the chapel through the other door, walking across the right side of the mosaic, which is similarly worn.

The baptistery remained in use from about AD 450 until perhaps as late as AD 650, when St Aldhelm (*d.*709) is thought to have established the small church that can be seen today, on a separate site above the river. The villa is set in Church Field, a name which may recall its earlier use; it is now a playing field in the grounds of St Laurence School. A small *chi-rho* pendant found at the ford over the River Avon at Bradford may have been worn by a Christian who worshipped at the villa house church.

The monastery of St Kea, Street

This is likely to lie beneath the parish church of Leigh, on the northern edge of the ancient town of Street. The name of the town, which is two miles southwest of Glastonbury, indicates that it was built on an ancient 'hard road'. It lay on the route from Glastonbury to the south, towards the ridge of the Polden Hills, and so to the estuary of the River Parrett. The causeway crosses some 600 metres of marshland surrounding the River Brue. In the eighteenth century a pre-Norman causeway was found under the turf, 12 metres east of the present road. It consisted of layers of stones set in brushwood, held in place by upright piles.[21]

The parish church, now dedicated to the Holy Trinity, was anciently claimed as one of Glastonbury's seven churches. Between the thirteenth and the sixteenth centuries it was dedicated to St Gildas. Also associated with the district, and from an earlier date, is the place name *Lantokay*, which appears in a grant of land by Bishop Haeddi of Winchester to the abbot of Glastonbury in 677–92. The name may be derived from St Kea, an obscure saint who, according to his *Life*, was born in Wales and migrated to Brittany.

Holy Trinity church, Street

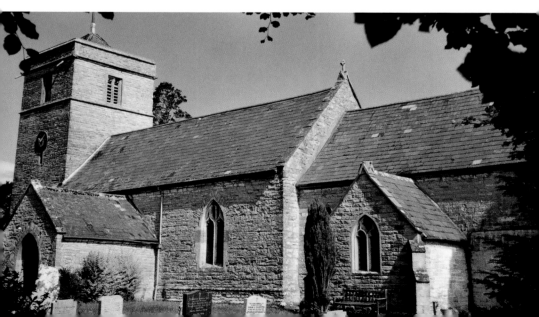

There is evidence of Kea's cult in Brittany, where his *Life* was written; Landkey in Devon and Old Kea in Cornwall (possibly the site of another early monastery) may also be named after him. At Landkey, the high banks of the churchyard outline the Celtic enclosure; its settlement was called *Landechei* in 1166, a name resembling that of Street's church. The Romano-British name of this saint derives from the Latin Caius, and he gave his name to Sir Kay, one of King Arthur's knights. Kea's feast day was celebrated on 5 November, and he was invoked for toothache.

The name *Lantokay* (church site of Kea) is the earliest recorded British *lan* site, predating those in Cornish and Welsh records by 200 years. The churchyard is a large oval enclosure, which tells us that this is likely to have contained a Celtic monastery. There was space for a cemetery surrounding the church, and dwellings for monks, craftsmen and labourers with their families. An earthwork inside its curved western boundary would have been the monastery's surrounding wall. The site had already been occupied: Roman potsherds, including Samian ware, and an Iron Age coin were found in the graveyard. An estate of three hides associated with the church was probably land tended by the monks.[22]

By the thirteenth century, the church had acquired a dependant chapel at Walton, two miles to the west. The name of this village means 'Welsh tun' or 'Foreigners' town', and denotes a British settlement in a predominantly Anglo-Saxon area. In 1503, the first enclosure beyond St Kea's church was known as *Ankerhey*, or 'anchorite's enclosure'. To the west of the church, old maps name a former manor house *Brutessayshe* (British ash); the ash was a holy tree in Celtic times. It is possible, therefore, that the first monks chose this site because it was already considered holy by the local people. Three ash trees were recorded as growing here in 1503.[23]

Across the River Brue, two miles from Street, there was a
Celtic hermitage on Glastonbury Tor, which may have been a
satellite of the monastery at Lantokay. Excavations on the Tor
conducted by Philip Rahtz (1964-6) revealed what may have
been monks' cells, cut into the rock below the summit in the
sixth century. Evidence was also found to suggest a tiny
Anglo-Saxon monastery on the site, with two monastic cells,
one of which was half underground, with a timber
superstructure. The location of this dwelling had been chosen
with some thought, for it was well-protected from the
prevailing winds, and had a pleasant view to the south.

In the layers dating from pre-Saxon times, Rahtz found
sherds of *amphorae*, perhaps containers for wine or olive oil,
imported from the Mediterranean. There were a great many
animal bones, mostly of cattle, with a few sheep or pigs. These
were the residue of joints brought to the site from animals
butchered elsewhere. The remains of so much meat led Rahtz
to at first conclude that this must have been a secular site,
perhaps a defended stronghold, until the discovery of large
quantities of meat bones at Whithorn and Iona provided
evidence that Celtic monks were meat-eaters.

There was a medieval tradition of a monastic foundation on
the Tor in early times, with two hermits. Two graves on the
Tor contained leg bones of young people, well under twenty
years old, of undetermined sex. There was a cairn, and two
metal-working hearths. Perhaps a product of this, a small
bronze carving of a face was found nearby, which may have
formed part of a pail handle, or even the head of a crosier.[24]

If there was a Saxon hermitage on the Tor, it would have
been a daughter house of the monastery below. On the Tor, a
timber church or communal building was built. In contrast to
the eating habits of their Celtic predecessors, the Saxon
occupants mainly ate birds (goose, domestic fowl, stock dove

*Bronze
head-mask,
Glastonbury Tor*

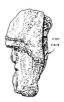

and corncrake) and fish (pike, perch, rudd, coalfish, hake and cod). Eggshells were found, but only eleven bones of sheep or cattle.[25] Saxon monks probably abstained from meat, except at Christmas and Easter.

The base of a tenth- or eleventh-century wheel cross, and what may have been its head, were found just below the summit of the Tor. The cross stood five feet high, tall enough to be visible from a distance. The ridges round the Tor indicate that it continued to be farmed in medieval times, for there was little land available for agriculture except for that on the steep-sided hills, since all the low-lying land was marsh. The present tower on the Tor was built in about 1360, following an earthquake which took place around 1300.

In Iron Age times, Glastonbury was an island, at least in winter. Lake Villages have been found in the marshland that surrounded it. The name Somerset indicates a region of summer pastures; in winter, when the land was flooded, the animals would have been slaughtered or moved to higher ground. When Morrison's superstore was being constructed to the west of the abbey, excavation by Charles and Nancy Hollinrake indicated a Roman civil settlement beneath the store's extensive car park. In the abbey grounds, they found

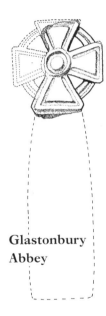

Glastonbury Abbey

Head of wheel-cross from the Anglo-Saxon monastery on the Tor

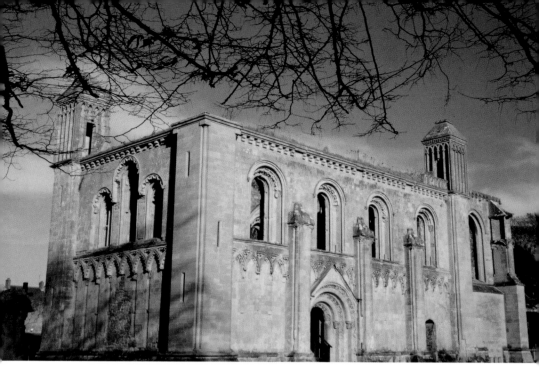

*Glastonbury
Abbey: the Lady
Chapel, consecrated
in 1186*

higher status Roman material, suggesting a villa on the site. The Hollinrakes also found Roman material on the Tor, where there was possibly a Roman temple, all traces of which would have been destroyed when the medieval church was built on the site.[26]

Since the earliest finds from excavations at the abbey date from the eighth century, it is likely to be of Saxon origin. There was probably a wooden church where the Lady Chapel now stands. A unique complex of glass furnaces dating from the late ninth or tenth century was associated with St Dunstan, who was interested in the technology of craft and industry, as well as being a gifted religious leader. The furnaces contained fragments of recycled Roman brick and tile. Glass vessels, beads and window glass were made, probably from re-used scrap. It is rare to find late Anglo-Saxon glass. Iron was also wrought here: *Domesday Book* records eight smiths attached to Glastonbury Manor.[27]

The present abbey ruins date from the eleventh century onwards. The enormous church and its surrounding buildings housed up to sixty men. Celtic monks including Kea, Fili, Rumon, Gildas and Collen were honoured here, but many of these dedications to the Celtic saints originated in the eleventh century, when the monks of Glastonbury created new interest in the lives of their Celtic predecessors.

In 1184 the great church was destroyed by fire. Glastonbury's superiority among English monasteries was threatened, and enterprising monastic historians developed a legend describing how Joseph of Arimathea, the disciple who buried Jesus in his family tomb, came to Glastonbury and built its first church. In 1191 the monks claimed to have discovered the tomb of King Arthur and his consort Guinevere beneath the floor of their church. The supposed relics of the royal couple were entombed in a shrine in the chancel in 1278.

Pilgrims approaching Glastonbury Abbey from the north travelled through Wells, and descended the steep hill into Glastonbury along the road named Bove Town. The final stopping place for pilgrims before they reached the abbey was St James' Chapel, now a private house named Jacobi Cottage. This was a 'slipper chapel' where pilgrims removed their shoes and washed their feet, before proceeding to the abbey on foot; the outline of its east window is still visible. The waters of a spring ran through a channel cut in the slabs that paved the floor. There were two similar chapels on the roads approaching the abbey from the south and the east. Jacobi House is named after St James of Compostella, another famous centre for pilgrimage.

On the southwestern edge of the town, Wearyall Hill is, according to medieval legend, the place where Joseph of Arimathea planted his staff. At the foot of Wearyall Hill, to

Glastonbury Tor
from Wearyall Hill,
with a cutting from
the Holy Thorn in
the foreground.

the north, there was a small Anglo-Saxon monastery at Beckery: it was a daughter house of Glastonbury Abbey, situated on a small low-lying hill whose summit was above the flood waters. It would have been the first stopping point for pilgrims travelling from the west, along the River Brue. In the early eighth century, Beckery became a focal point for Irish monks as they passed to and fro from Ireland to mainland Europe.[28]

**St Indract
(Shapwick):
murdered for
a sack of
celery seed**

Shapwick Heath

Oone of the many Celtic saints whose relics were claimed
by the medieval monks of Glastonbury was St Indract.
His story may be genuine: the Irish *Martyrology of Tallaght*,
written around AD 800, describes him as 'a martyr for the faith
at Glastonbury'. He was possibly an abbot of Iona, or of
Kells in County Meath, where the monks of Iona later settled,
in a location better protected from Norse raids than the isle
of Iona.

According to Indract's twelfth-century *Life*, which its author says he has derived from an old English source, Indract was the son of an Irish prince. When he was a deacon, he visited Rome with twelve companions. On the way home, bringing sacks of celery seed, presumably to plant in his monastery, the little group visited Glastonbury. They stayed for the night near Shapwick, which is just north of the Polden ridge, on an ancient route from Glastonbury to the coast.

Excavations at Old Church Farm, Shapwick, 2000

Here, a thegn of the King of Wessex murdered Indract and his companions, thinking that their sacks contained gold. Indract was buried at Shapwick, which was the mother church of the area. Indract's relics were taken to Glastonbury Abbey, where they were enshrined beside the high altar of the old church, which was destroyed in the great fire of 1184.[29]

The original site of the village is at Old Church Farm, half a mile out of Shapwick, east of the present church. Excavation here has provided evidence of Roman settlement and of a large medieval building lower down the field from the site of the former church.

Pattern on a bronze boss from the Polden Hills, Somerset.

A Roman road ran from the Fosse Way past Shapwick to the sea. There was a Romano-British villa at Shapwick, and in 1988 Britain's largest hoard of early Roman coins was found here. It was buried around AD 230, and was the equivalent of about ten years' pay for a legionary soldier.[30] Had the Saxon thegns been better informed, they might not have gone to the trouble of murdering Indract! Near the church there was evidence of a Bronze Age hut, and a large spring emerged on the east side of the church. This site had experienced continuous settlement over a long period. In medieval times the villagers moved to a new location, half a mile west of their original settlement. This is where the present fourteenth-century church can be found.

St Cyngar (Congresbury): a shrine in the marshes

Of the Celtic saints who are said to have worked in Somerset, Cyngar is the most likely to have existed. He gave his name to Congresbury, and may have been associated with the nearby hill fort of Cadbury, 3/4 of a mile to the north.

This is one of five camps in the southwest to be named 'Cadbury' or 'Cada's fort'. It was probably occupied by members of the Dobuni tribe, who were based in the Cotswolds. The fort was abandoned during the Roman occupation, from AD 43 to 410, when the lowland around it was under stable Roman administration, as the region grew and flourished. However, the hill fort gained a new lease of life, and was reoccupied from around AD 410 until AD 700. Perhaps it was now no longer safe to live in the lowlands below the fort.

St Congar's Walking Stick in Congresbury churchyard

Cadbury camp is the only fortress in the region to have been lived in once again after the departure of the Romans. *Amphorae* were found here, still imported from Mediterranean lands, as they had been in Roman times. The people living here were wealthy: the fort has produced Britain's second largest collection of fragments of early medieval glass. There were at least sixty vessels; the only site to produce more is Whithorn, which yielded pieces of some eighty vessels.[31]

It is possible that the monk Cyngar lived near the people in the fort, for on the adjacent hilltop of Henley Hill at Yatton is what appears to have been an early Christian cemetery. There had been a Roman temple here which fell into ruin in the third century, and later, perhaps in the sixth century, between fifty and a hundred Christian graves were dug through the site. Unfortunately, the site has now been quarried away.

In Saxon times, the settlement of Congresbury grew alongside the River Yeo which flows at the foot of the fort, a mile to the southwest. Here there was a minster church and a monastery. The large oblong site of ten acres is bounded by deep ditches, and probably dates from the seventh century. There was a second church within the enclosure, dedicated to St Michael. Since the Archangel Michael is associated with the souls of the dead, this was probably a mortuary chapel.

In 1996, in the floor of a barn at Brinsea near Congresbury, stones were discovered which had formed part of Cyngar's eleventh-century shrine, including a piece of one of its corner pillars. It would have been a substantial monument, over two metres high. Two sculptured figures depict Christ and a tonsured saint, perhaps St Peter. A large torso fragment may have come from a statue of Cyngar.[32] The sculptures are now in Taunton Museum. The shrine probably stood near or behind the high altar of the minster church.

Cyngar's cult may have waned, for in 1217/18 the church was rebuilt and rededicated to St Andrew. The great east window was constructed at this time. St Cyngar's shrine was now seen to be in the way, and his relics were relegated to a side chapel off the south aisle, where the arched recess of his tomb can still be seen. Some of the stone foundations of his shrine were re-used in the new east wall of the church, which was rebuilt yet again in the fourteenth and fifteenth centuries. In the churchyard, an ancient yew stump inside a beech tree is still known as 'Congar's Walking Stick.

Figures from St Cyngar's shrine: a tonsured saint above the head of Christ

Cyngar was said to have planted his staff here, where it took root, and this miracle persuaded the Saxon King Ine of

Wessex to grant land for a monastery. Even today, yew is a traditional wood for carving walking sticks.

Cyngar may have been a Welsh monk. The improbable medieval *Life of Cyngar* tells of a dream in which a wild boar shows Cyngar where he should live. On waking, he sees a boar in a reed bed, and builds an oratory on the site. A wild boar features in a number of Celtic saints' *Lives*: often a white sow indicates where a monk's chief monastery should be built. Swineherds lived on the edge of settlements, where a monk could combine solitude with accessibility to local people. Medieval Christians familiar with the classics would recall that a huge white sow showed Aeneas where to found the great city of Alba Longa, the forerunner of Rome.[33]

Congresbury is first mentioned in Asser's *Life of Alfred* as a derelict Celtic monastery that King Alfred assigned to Asser, Bishop of Crediton. Eleventh- and fourteenth-century pilgrim guides describe Cyngar's body enshrined in the church. Next to the church there is a fine thirteenth century priests' house, built to accommodate the clerics who ministered to the pilgrims visiting the shrine.

The Yeo Valley, Congresbury

St Kew (Kewstoke): a baptistery by the sea

St Kew is a little-known female Celtic saint who may be commemorated in the village of Kewstoke, on the Somerset coast, a mile northeast of Weston-super-Mare. Since she is relatively obscure, it is unlikely that Kew's cult owes its origin to later medieval interest in famous Celtic saints of the past. At Kewstoke, the church and graveyard form part of a roughly oval enclosure, which appears to predate the surrounding landscape; this suggests the presence of a small religious community here in Celtic times. In *Domesday Book* (1186), Kewstoke appears as *Chiwestoch*. The suffix *stoc* is an Old English place name element which can mean 'a religious place'. It sometimes appears as 'stow' or 'stoke', to replace the lost British name of an early church site.[34]

The small parish church at Kewstoke is now dedicated to St Paul; no record survives of an earlier dedication to St Kew. The late medieval church may reflect an Anglo-Saxon design, in its dimensions, height and floor plan. Saxon openings may have been enlarged to become what are rather unusual clerestory windows. A remarkable flight of steps leads from the churchyard up the steep cliff of Worlebury Hill. It is now known as Monk's Steps, but on earlier maps the flight is named St Kew's Steps. A century ago, they rose dramatically between the bare rock face on either side of a gully, but the hillside is now gently wooded.

On a platform halfway up St Kew's Steps are the remains of a stone building 6 x 4 metres in size, enclosing a pit which was probably a well. This appears to have been an early well chapel or baptistery. When it was excavated in the late nineteenth century, finds suggested ritual use in the Iron Age; it continued to be frequented until the late medieval period. A rare piece of early British metalwork, a penannular silver brooch, was found in 1853 at the top of the steps. The closest parallel to this site is at St Levan in Cornwall, near Land's

OPPOSITE:
St Kew's Steps, Kewstoke

End, where the remains of two stone structures, said to be St Selevan's chapel and cell, are connected by an ancient flight of over sixty stone steps to a holy well and baptistery, higher up the cliff.

There are two other dedications to St Kew: Llangiwa in Monmouthshire and St Kew near Padstow in Cornwall, where she is connected with Docco. A charter of Edgar dating from AD 961 refers to the monastery of St Dochou and St Cywa.[35] This Cornish community is the monastery where, according to his seventh-century *Life*, St Samson hoped to stay with his companions, but was dissuaded from doing so by its monks, apparently because they had grown lax, and did not want to incur Bishop Samson's disapproval. We shall never know whether a small group of nuns from this community settled at Kewstoke.

St Maildubh of Malmesbury

The name Maildubh means 'black monk' or 'black servant, since *mael* means 'tonsured servant' and *dubh* means 'black'. According to medieval tradition, Maildubh was an Irish monk who established a small community and a school for noblemen's sons at Malmesbury. The Saxon monk Aldhelm was his most outstanding pupil and became his successor. However, Aldhelm makes no mention of Maildubh in his prose works or poetry, and we hear nothing of the Irish monk until 400 years after Aldhelm's death. The earliest histories of Malmesbury are those of Faricius of Arezzo (*d.*1117) who lived at Malmesbury between 1080 and 1100, when he was appointed abbot of Abingdon, and by William of Malmesbury (*c*1090–1143).

William describes Maildubh as an 'Irishman by birth, a philosopher by erudition and a monk by profession,' who left Ireland in search of a solitary life. Although historians have cast doubt on Maildubh's existence, his story is not unlikely. Aldhelm himself tells us little about his own life, and nothing

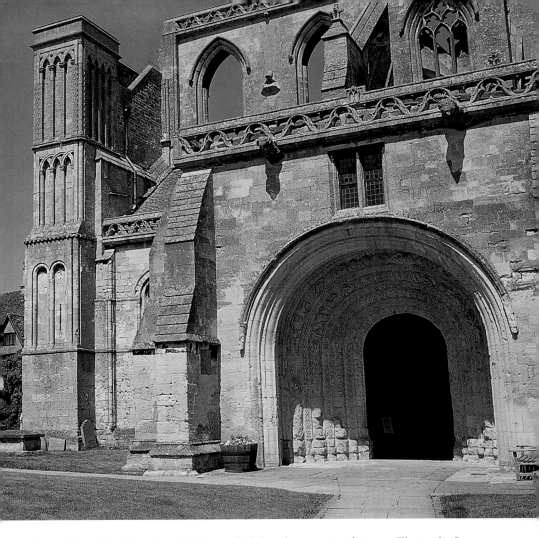

The porch of Malmesbury Abbey

about his early education. William of Malmesbury notes that, on account of Viking raids, the abbey library lacked information about Aldhelm, so William's account was written largely from oral history.

Malmesbury is an ancient settlement: in 2000 a previously unknown Iron Age town was discovered beneath modern Malmesbury. It was forty acres in size, and encircled by stone ramparts over three metres wide. The town was built between

the fifth and second centuries BC, and was strongly fortified. The settlement was probably the main centre of a tribal group that eventually federated with its neighbours to become the kingdom of the Dobuni.

The Iron Age town was built on high ground within a loop of the River Avon, with a few hundred inhabitants sheltering behind 1.5 metres of stone defences. They lived in round

houses of stone or timber, with roofs of thatch. They farmed, and the settlement was perhaps the chief economic centre of the southeast Cotswolds. Radiating out from it is a 30-mile cluster of Iron Age farms and settlements, as aerial photography shows.[36]

The medieval town wall partly follows that of its Iron Age predecessor. Although Malmesbury stopped being a

Panel depicting six apostles, in Malmesbury Abbey porch

significant centre of population from about 100 BC to AD 800, it may have continued as a religious centre. There was possibly a small Romano-British temple beneath the abbey, dedicated to a local deity. This would be an obvious place for Christian monks to establish a community and a centre of learning.

The Saxons conquered this area in the sixth century, after a victory at Dyrham near Bath, and Malmesbury became part of the kingdom of the West Saxons. Aldhelm became abbot of Malmesbury in about 675. The south church of the abbey may survive from his seventh-century church. Over the door, the tympanum depicts Christ enthroned, with supporting angels. Each side wall contains a panel of six apostles with an angel flying overhead. The rest of the south porch, with its bands of stone carving, dates from the twelfth or thirteenth century; it is one of the finest in Europe.

ecuman is the patron saint of the small settlement at St
Decumans, a mile southwest of Watchet on the north
Somerset coast. He is thought to have been a sixth-century
Welsh monk, possibly from Brecon. He may have given his
name to a monastery at Rhoscrowther (formerly named
Llanddegyman) in Pembrokeshire. This community was of
some significance, since it is named in *The Laws of Howel the*

**St Decuman
(Watchet): a
famous holy
well**

*Semicircular pool,
St Decuman's well*

Good as one of the 'seven bishop houses in Dyved', alongside the great monasteries of St David's, Llandeilo Fawr and others. Decuman's name suggests that he was a Romanised Briton (*Decumanus* is Latin for 'tenth').

Decuman is another example of an obscure Somerset saint whose church dedication is unlikely to be the result of later medieval interest. His fifteenth-century *Life* was probably written at Wells cathedral, to which St Decumans belonged. It relates that he lived as a hermit near Dunster, and was murdered one day while at prayer. Like St Nectan and others, after being beheaded, he picked up his head and walked to the spring which flows fifty metres northwest of the church, where his life blood conferred healing properties on the water. In Celtic thought, the head, rather than the heart, was regarded as the source of life. These stories were told to demonstrate the saint's power over death.

The spring is down a lane, on the steeply sloping hillside. It is covered by a circular well house, and a little lower down the slope, the water flows into two semicircular basins before going underground. A record from around 1100 states: 'The fountain of St Decumanus is sweet, healthful, and necessary to the inhabitants for drinking purposes'. A Byzantine coin from the mint of Constantinople was found in 'St Decuman's Garden', which may have been the area around the well. The coin was a *follis* of Justinian I (AD 540–41); it was more likely to have been used as jewellery than as money.[37]

St Decumans church tower is a landmark visible from some distance, both from the sea and overland. Across the valley of the Washford River, overlooking the sea, there is likely to have been an early church associated with the nearby Anglo-Saxon *burh* at Daw's Castle. One of these two churches may have replaced the other, or both may have co-existed. A field at Daw's Castle is named 'Minster Field', which suggests an

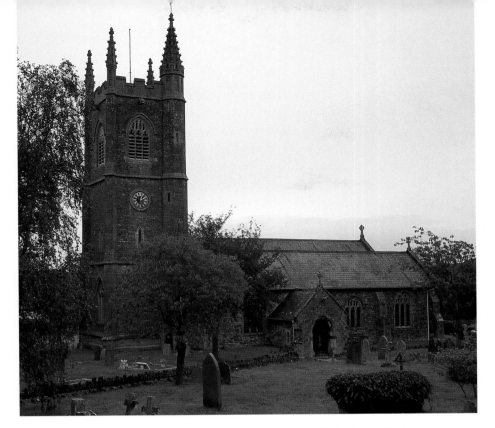

Carhampton Church

Anglo–Saxon minster, perhaps on the site of a British monastery. The church at St Decumans was of some importance in Saxon times: it was located on the royal estate of Williton, where it had a dependant chapel in about 1175. In 1190 St Decumans was given to Wells cathedral; the present church dates from the late thirteenth century.[38]

St Carantoc (Carhampton): a monastery is excavated

Carantoc is said to have lived in a cave above the church named after him at Llangrannog on the Ceredigion coast. Two medieval *Lives* of St Carantoc survive in a manuscript in the British Library, dating from around AD 1200. The first *Life* relates how he came from Ceredigion and founded one or more churches in Britain. The second *Life* connects the saint with the story of how Cunedda and his sons expelled the Irish from Ceredigion.

Little information survives about Carantoc's cult. The most significant foundation named after him is at Crantock on the north Cornish coast: in *Domesday Book*, Crantock is referred to as *Langorroc*, using a hypocoristic, or pet form of Carantoc's name. In the sixteenth century, the antiquarian Nicholas Roscarrock related that seven parishes used to bring relics each year to the seven churchyards of Crantock in procession, and each relic was placed on a stone altar.[39]

Another medieval church was dedicated to Carantoc at Carhampton in Somerset. Its place name is formed from the Old English words *carrum* and *tun* ('rock town'), but the sixteenth-century antiquary John Leland thought that the place name derived from the saint. By that time it was known as *Carntoun*, which he explained as 'Carantokes towne'. Leland describes two churches, one being the church of St John the Baptist that survives today, and the other 'a chapel of this sainct [Carantoc] that sumtyme was the paroch chirche'.[40]

The location of Carantoc's church remained unknown until 1993, when Charles and Nancy Hollinrake excavated an early medieval building at Eastbury Farm on the eastern edge of the village. The site is typical of a Celtic monastery, in an undefended location, on the edge of the alluvial levels, with easy access to the sea. There are suitable landing bays and beaches within half a mile, yet its location renders it invisible to pirates. Unfortunately, torrential rains hindered the Hollinrakes' exploratory excavations, but nevertheless, significant discoveries were made.

Most of the features investigated dated from the sixth to the tenth centuries: timber buildings, a cemetery, and enclosures bounded by ditches. There were four pieces of sixth-century pottery imported from the Mediterranean, including the handle of an *amphora*, and a piece of seventh-century imported pottery, probably from Gaul.

Two fragments of early glass were also found: all these artefacts suggest a high status site. Nearby was an enclosed cemetery, in use from the twelfth to the sixteenth centuries. All this probably lay within a large oval enclosure, about 350 metres long and 250 metres wide.[41]

The position of the early medieval church was deduced from holes for posts, stakes and perhaps timbers. There were early cobbled floors and possible cobbled tracks. A number of finds dated from the fourth and fifth centuries, suggesting that this was a very early site. Its most unusual feature was a large quantity of iron ore and slag. Iron was smelted here, mainly in the sixth and seventh centuries, but continuing into the tenth century. Some of the iron may have been used for smithing in the monastery, but most of it was worked into billets for export. This is the only early British smelting site in the southwest of England; it could be one of the largest so far discovered in England and Wales.[42]

In Saxon times, the three royal estates of Carhampton, Williton and Cannington encompassed the entire northwest Somerset coast between Minehead and the River Parrett. The Anglo-Saxon Chronicle records successful Danish raids on Carhampton in the ninth century; the site would have been easy to capture if Carhampton were an undefended monastery. Despite the raids, it continued to be occupied through the Saxon period into the thirteenth century, unlike many other Celtic sites in Western Britain.[43] It is tantalising that so much has been discovered from exploratory trenches which were cut prior to the creation of a village bypass that was never constructed.

An important Romano-British monk and bishop, Dubricius (d.*c*550) has a number of dedications in Hereford and Gwent. His mother was a chieftain's daughter from the small territory of Erging in Herefordshire. He was said to have

St Dubricius (Porlock): an early bishop

been born at Madley near Hereford, and his chief monastery was at Hentland, near Ross-on-Wye.

The seventh-century *Life of Samson* presents Dubricius as a prominent figure among the Christians of south Wales; he was perhaps the equivalent of a later archbishop, his authority extending over more than one kingdom. The *Life of Samson* relates that Dubricius appointed Samson as abbot of the community on Caldey Island, two miles south of Tenby. Dubricius is said to have retired to Bardsey Island in old age and to have died there.

The church at Porlock is named *Ecclesia S. Dubricii* in the foundation deed of the Harrington chantry in 1476, and it is

Remains of ancient yew tree, Porlock churchyard

OPPOSITE:
Rood screen, Timberscombe church

not known how early this dedication might be. Porlock would have been a day's sail from the great monasteries of south Wales. The skeleton of an ancient yew tree stands in the churchyard, so this may be a pre-Christian holy site. Inside the church are two pieces of a pre-Norman cross, the earliest surviving stone carving from the churches of west Somerset. Porlock's church was formerly closer to the sea, which has now receded. It was restored in the fifteenth century, and again in the nineteenth century. Its stocky tower, dating from around the thirteenth century, may have had a light on top of its spire, to guide boats into the harbour.

There are several churches near Porlock which were probably dedicated to Celtic saints in late medieval times. One is the tiny chapel of Culbone, which lies along a wooded footpath on the coast two miles north-northwest of Porlock; this could be named after the Irish missionary, St Columbanus. Another example is Timberscombe, halfway between Porlock and St Decuman's, which acquired Petroc as its patron saint because it was owned by Bodmin priory, where St Petroc was honoured. His magnificent medieval reliquary can still be seen in Bodmin church.

Timberscombe's name means 'timber valley', and its church is one of several in the area with a magnificent medieval rood screen carved from local oak, perhaps felled in the valley. The photo shows the middle portion of the screen, with its imitation stone tracery and fan vaulting. A rood screen separated the priest in the chancel from the congregation, who sat in the nave; it was topped with a cross, or rood. There were skilled carvers at nearby Dunster Abbey, who worked in the surrounding area: a similar rood screen can be seen at Carhampton.

Susan Pearce has identified another ten possible early British churches in Somerset, with seven more in Dorset and a further twenty-two in Devon.[44] For most of these, all trace of their founder has been lost. Some were later named after Celtic saints who were popular throughout the Middle Ages, such as Bridestowe and Virginstow in Devon, both named after St Bridget of Kildare. However, there are three early sites near the Somerset coast dedicated to Bridget where it is possible that the Celtic goddess Brígh was formerly honoured.

Brígh appears to have been the titular deity of the Brigantes, the largest confederacy of tribes in Britain. This was the dominant tribe in northern England before the arrival of the Romans. The Brigantes were also found in Switzerland near Lake Constance, where the town of Bregenz is named after them. The Celtic word *brigā* means 'high one' or 'high place'. Living in their hill forts, the Brigantes were successful warriors, and those whom they defeated coined the word 'brigand' to describe their unwelcome presence.

Brean Down: from temple to parish church

Two miles southwest of Weston-super-Mare is the village of Brean, whose church is dedicated to St Bridget. Nearer to Weston-super-Mare, the headland of Brean Down marks the western end of the Mendip Hills. The name Brean derives from the Celtic word *Brigantia*; it may be that Brígh was honoured on the Down before Bridget was commemorated in the church below.

Until medieval times, Brean Down was an island; people lived, farmed and worshipped on the Down for four thousand years. A Romano-Celtic temple was built here in about AD 340; it appears to have been in use for only thirty years. There is an extensive sub-Roman cemetery on the shoulder of Brean Down, one of six so far discovered in Somerset. Its graves appear tantalisingly from time to time in the eroding

*Brean Down: a
Bronze Age village
lies beneath the
gently shelving bay*

*The Roman temple
on Brean Down*

sand cliff. Remains from the graves have been carbon-dated to around AD 410.

The temple on the Down above was partly demolished in order to build what appears to have been a Christian church, on an east-west axis. Coins found here indicate that this building was in use during the fifth century.[45] A further five graves dating from the fifth to the seventh century were discovered nearby. These too were oriented east-west in the Christian manner.

In 1976 Dr Martin Bell of Lampeter University found the footings of round stone houses and bones and pottery dating from the Bronze Age, out in the flat land 100–200 metres offshore, showing that sea level was lower in earlier times than it is today. Perhaps this was the site of the original village of Brean.[46] The first Christian church and its cemetery would have been nearby. In later medieval times, the village and its church may have been rebuilt on higher ground further south, where they remain today.

Brent Knoll: a hill fort and a holy well

Five miles southeast of Brean Down, another 'high place' named Brent Knoll rises above the marshes. Early forms of the word Brent are *Briente* and *Brunte*.

These suggest a Celtic name derived from *Brigantia*. There is a roughly triangular Iron Age hill fort on the summit of Brent Knoll, in which early excavations indicated a temple where Brígh may have been honoured; fragments of its wall plaster were found. An Iron Age spindle whorl suggested the presence of family dwellings. The Romans later occupied the fort: Roman silver and copper coins were found on the summit, and fragments of red Samian ware.

The fort was subsequently used by the Anglo-Saxons as a refuge against marauding Danes. Its interior has been damaged by quarrying for lias limestone which caps the hill, and trenches inside the fort were adapted for use by military personnel in the Second World War. In medieval times, the population moved down to the site of the present village on the shoulder of the Knoll. Here one of a line of springs used for drinking water by the villagers was formerly known as 'Our Lady's well'; this title often refers to St Bridget.[47]

Brent Knoll in winter

Chelvey is an early church site dedicated to Bridget, which may once have been named after the goddess Brígh; it is in a small village eight miles southwest of Bristol. Like the previous two sites, it occupies a prominent position, being set on a low hill, with views over the surrounding countryside. Chelvey manor is mentioned in *Domesday Book* (1086), so the adjacent church was probably also in existence. The north wall of the nave is Norman; so too is the arch over the south door and the font: these date from about 1140. The church was rebuilt in the thirteenth century; a tall preaching cross stands in the churchyard. St Bridget was patroness of smithing, and next to Chelvey church, local smiths work over their furnace, although Bridget would not recognise the iron bedsteads which they produce.

St Bridget's church, Chelvey: the south porch and preaching cross

Bridget's cult is one of the clearest examples of the fusion of a Christian saint with elements of earlier religious belief, but lack of evidence means that we know little about pre-Christian worship or beliefs in Wessex. The documentation of Celtic Christianity in this region is also somewhat sketchy, and not until the Saxon period can we form a clearer picture of churches, monasteries and their local saints. Bishop Asser's *Life of Alfred* and other texts provide vivid eye-witness accounts of the growth of the Church in Wessex. Finally, with the systematic description of each town and village, and its surrounding land in *Domesday Book*, the Normans documented the parish system which has largely survived until today.

Notes

1. B Cunliffe *The Roman Baths at Bath* Bath Archaeological Trust, 1993, pp3–9
2. D Petts *Christianity in Roman Britain* Tempus, Stroud, 2003, p.41
3. *Meet the Ancestors* Series, BBC TV Channel 2, December 2000, presented by Julian Richards, produced by Suzanne Daggar
4. B Cunliffe *op. cit.*, pp.30–31, 35
5. P Leach *Shepton Mallet: Romano-Britons and Early Christians in Somerset* Birmingham University Field Archaeology Unit, 1991, pp.9, 24
6. D Petts *op. cit.*, p.140
7. M Costen *The Origins of Somerset* Manchester University Press, 1992, p.62
8. *Ibid* p.76
9. M Corney *The Roman Villa at Bradford on Avon: The Investigations of 2003*, Ex Libris Press, Bradford on Avon, 2003, p.19
10. J Toynbee 'Pagan Motifs and Practices in Christian Art and Ritual' in M W Barley and R P Hanson (eds) *Christianity in Britain, 300–700*, Leicester University Press, 1968, pp.180–86
11. D Perring 'Gnosticism in fourth-century Britain: the Frampton mosaics reconsidered' in *Britannia – A Journal of Romano-British and Kindred Studies* vol.xxxiv, 2003, p.97
12. J Toynbee *op. cit.*, p.185
13. D Perring *op. cit.*, p.105
14. *Ibid.*, p.109
15. J Toynbee *op. cit.*, p.182
16. *Ibid.*
17. D Perring *op. cit.*, p.113
18. R Goodman *The Roman Villa, Chedworth* National Trust, London 1994, p.24
19. D Perring *op. cit.*, p.113
20. M Corney *op. cit.*, p.18
21. P Rahtz *The English Heritage Book of Glastonbury* Batsford/English Heritage, London, 1991, p.112
22. M Calder 'Early ecclesiastical sites in Somerset: three case studies' *Proceedings of the Somerset Archaeological and Natural History Society* 147, 2004, pp.4–7
23. P Rahtz *op. cit.*, p.30
24. *Ibid.*, pp.54–7
25. *Ibid.*, p.60
26. Conversation with N and C Hollinrake, 2004
27. P Rahtz *op. cit.*, pp.91–2

28. *Ibid.*, pp.118–9
29. M Lapidge 'The cult of St Indract at Glastonbury' in *Ireland and Early Medieval Europe: Studies in memory of Kathleen Hughes* ed. D Whitelock, R McKitterick and D Dumville, Cambridge University Press, 1982, pp.184–8
30. D Millward 'Finders keep Roman coins' in *The Daily Telegraph*, 10 November 1999
31. P Hill *Whithorn and St Ninian: the Excavation of a Monastic Town* Sutton Publishing, Stroud, 1997, p.297
32. C Oakes and M Costen 'The Congresbury carvings – an Eleventh-Century Saint's Shrine?' in *The Antiquaries Journal* vol.83, 2003, pp.281–309
33. K Jankulak 'Alba Longa in the Celtic regions? Swine, saints and Celtic hagiography' in *Celtic Hagiography and Saints, 2000* ed. J Cartwright, University of Wales Press, Cardiff, 2003, pp.271–84
34. M Calder *op. cit.*, pp.11–16
35. *Ibid.*
36. D Keys 'Archaeologists find Iron Age gateway to the Cotswolds' in *The Independent*, 5 June, 2000
37. M Calder *op cit.*, pp.15–24
38. *Ibid.*
39. K Jankulak *Carantoc alias Cairnech? British saints, Irish saints and the Irish in Wales,* a paper presented at the annual Conference of the Celtic Studies Association of North America, Toronto, 2004
40. *Ibid.*
41. C and N Hollinrake *Archaeological Evaluations at Carhampton, Somerset, 1993–1994,* unpublished
42. *Ibid.*
43. *Ibid.*
44. S Pearce *The Kingdom of Dumnonia – Studies in History and Tradition in South Western Britain AD 350–1150* Lodenek Press, Padstow, Cornwall, 1978, pp.182–5
45. P Rahtz 'Sub-Roman Cemeteries in Somerset' in *Christianity in Britain 300–700, op. cit.* p.194
46. J Jackman *Brean: The Millenium Years* Square One Publications, Upton-on-Severn, Worcestershire, 1999, p.2
47. M Costen *op. cit.*, p.46

Index